LA HISTÒRIA DELS NÚMEROS

THE NUMBER STORY

SMALL BOOK ONE

ENGLISH - CATALAN

Numbers Teach Children
Their Number Names

written and illustrated by

MISS ANNA

Early Reader Edition of *The Number Story 1*
Bronze Medal Winner, 2016 Wishing Shelf Book Award

Cover by | Lumpy Publishing
Layout by | Lumpy Publishing
Translated by Xavi and Sachi
Coloring by Jieeun Woo and Maria Mirabella

Library of Congress Control Number: 2018902040

Names: Miss Anna, author.
Title: Number story : numbers teach children their number names / Miss Anna.
Description: Portland, OR: Lumpy Publishing, 2018.
Identifiers: ISBN 978-0-9962164-1-8 | LCCN 2018902040
Summary: The pictures and rhymes present stories which introduce numbers 0-10.
Subjects: LCSH Numeration—English--Catalan--Pictorial works--Juvenile literature. | BISAC JUVENILE NONFICTION /
Languages: English--Catalan
Classification: LCC QA141.3 .M57 2018 | DDC 513—dc23

Publisher: Lumpy Publishing
Website: www.missannabooks.com
Email: missanna@missannabooks.com

Paperback: ISBN 978-0-9962164-1-8
Printed in the U.S.A.   1 3 5 7 9 10 8 6 4 2

Vols aprendre els noms
dels números?

It is very easy and a lot of fun!

És molt fàcil i molt divertit!

Say-along our little jingle

Canta amb nosaltres la nostra petita història!

starting from Number One!

Comencem des del número u!

1

ONE looks like my one finger.

U

sembla el meu dit.

ONE!
U!

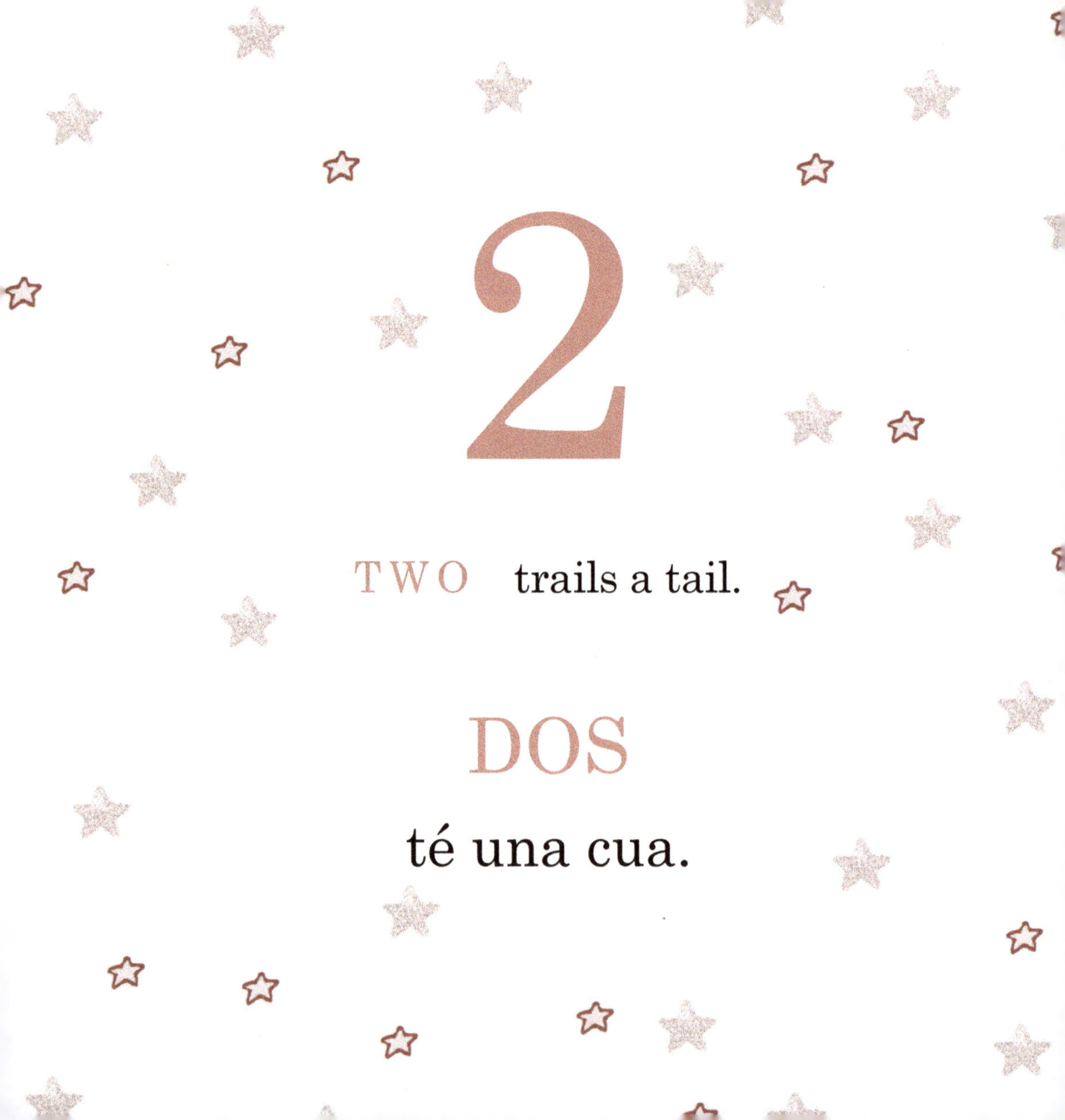

2
TWO trails a tail.
DOS
té una cua.

A TAIL! UNA CUA!

3

THREE   has bumps.

TRES

té bonys.

Abonyegat! Mira els bonys!

4

FOUR carries a sail.

QUATRE

té una vela.

4
A SAIL!
UNA VELA!

5

FIVE is a racing track.

CINC

és una pista de carreres.

VROOM
RUUUM!
1

6

S I X curves like a snail.

SIS

es doblega com un cargol.

A SNAIL!   UN CARGOL!

7

SEVEN has a sharp angle.

SET

té un angle afilat.

BE CAREFUL! IT'S SHARP!

Ves amb compte! Està Afilat!

8

EIGHT   is rollercoaster rails.

VUIT

és un rail de muntanya russa.

YUUHUU!
YIPPEE!

NINE is a bubble on a stick.

NOU

és una bombolla en un pal.

A BUBBLE! UNA BOMBOLLA!

10
TEN is an eye of a whale.
DEU
és un ull d'una balena.

HELLO!
HOLA!

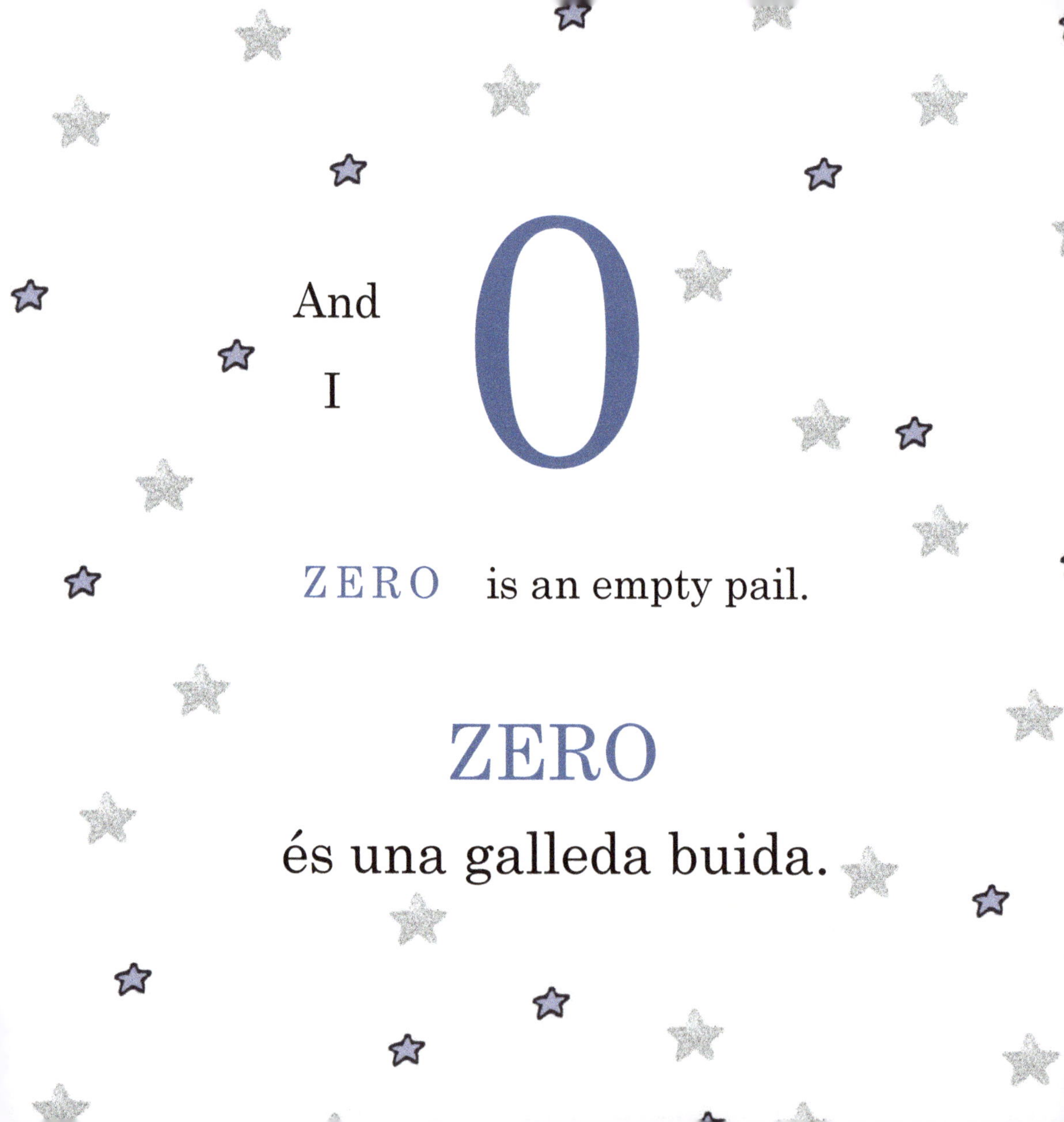

And I
O
ZERO is an empty pail.
ZERO
és una galleda buida.

IT'S EMPTY!
ÉS BUIT!

Thank you for playing with us today.

We had a lot of fun too!

Gràcies per jugar amb nosaltres avui.

Ens em divertit molt també!

We are your Number friends,
Zero to Ten,
Who will be here for you~
Som els teus amics
de Zero a Deu.

Estarem sempre aquí per tu.

Bye-bye now!
See you again soon!
Fins aviat!
Ens veiem!

The Numbers are *SINGING* too!

To sing-a-long, look for Miss Anna Number Story
at your favorite music store like iTUNES.

MP3

Numbers 0-10
IDENTIFYING & COUNTING

Numbers 11-20
& Ordinals
first, second, third...

Numbers 0-100
& Place Values
ones, tens, hundreds...

About Clocks
& Telling Time
hours, minutes, seconds

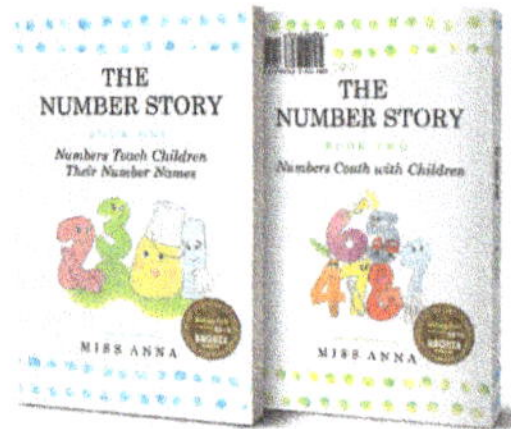

Number Story 1 & 2
isbn: 978-0-996216-48-7

Number Story 3 & 4
isbn: 978-1-945977-01-5

Number Story 5 & 6
isbn: 978-1-945977-06-0

Number Story 7 & 8
isbn: 978-1-949320-40-4

For more Miss Anna books to love,
visit us at

www.missannabooks.com

Numbers are working hard all over the world!
Come Travel the World with Us!